MISSISSIPPI DELTA

NATURAL WONDERS

Jason Cooper

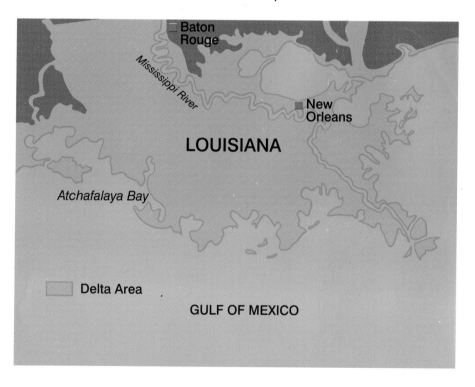

The Rourke Press, Inc.
Vero Beach, Florida 32964

PHOTO CREDITS
Cover, pages 13 and 17, © James P. Rowan; page 10 coutesy of NASA; page 18 © Lynn M. Stone; pages 4, 7, 8, 12,15, 21 courtesy Louisiana Office of Tourism

Library of Congress Cataloging-in-Publication Data

Cooper, Jason, 1942-
   Mississippi Delta / Jason Cooper
      p. cm. — (Natural Wonders)
   Includes index.
   ISBN 1-57103-016-6
    1. Mississippi River Delta (La.)—Juvenile literature.
I. Title II. Series: Cooper, Jason, 1942-   Natural Wonders.
F377.M6C66   1995
917.7' 0946—dc20   95–12305
                                        CIP
                                        AC

Printed in the USA

TABLE OF CONTENTS

THE MISSISSIPPI DELTA

The Mississippi River **delta** (DEL tuh) is a broad, low land that the river itself has made near its mouth. The Mississippi's mouth is in southern Louisiana, where the river meets the Gulf of Mexico.

The Mississippi delta covers an area about the size of Connecticut and Massachusetts combined. Delta land accounts for about one-quarter of the state of Louisiana.

Mississippi River delta country is a jigsaw puzzle of land and water

DELTA COUNTRY

Much of the delta is wetland—land that is under water at least part of the time. The Mississippi delta also has forests, farms, towns, and cities.

The most famous city is New Orleans, known for its food, jazz music, and a winter festival called **Mardi Gras** (MAR de GRAH).

South and west of New Orleans are miles of delta marshes, wooded swamps, and fertile fields. Snaky channels of blackwater called **bayous** (BUY youz) twist through the delta.

New Orleans, on the banks of the Mississippi River, is one of America's best-known cities

THE MISSISSIPPI RIVER

The Mississippi River delta is huge because the mighty river is a tremendous land-building force.

The Mississippi River is the longest river in the United States. Its 2,340-mile length drains water from states as distant as Montana and New York. It has the fourth biggest drainage system of any river in the world.

With its great volume of water, "Old Man River" carries a huge amount of **sediment** (SEHD uh mint).

Brown with sediment, the mighty Mississippi winds toward the ocean

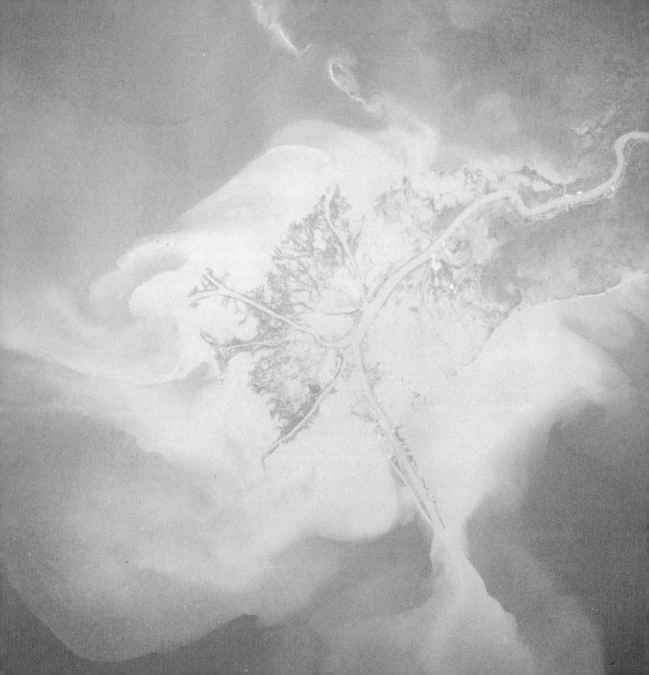

BUILDING THE DELTA

Sediments are particles of clay, gravel, sand and other solids. A river's movement, or current, sweeps sediments along with it.

When a river reaches the ocean, its current slows, as if it has hit a wall. The sediments are no longer being carried by fast-moving water, so they sink.

Slowly, they build up, making new land near a river's mouth. Natural flooding by a river is part of the process.

This is a satellite view of the
Mississippi winding toward the ocean

Shrimp boats are common sights in delta harbors

Freshwater swamps on the delta support a variety of wildlife

THE CHANGING DELTA

The Mississippi River is extremely useful. When it floods, it can be extremely dangerous.

The river is somewhat tamed in Louisiana—and elsewhere—by dams and canals. For example, a large portion of the Mississippi's natural flow in Louisiana is forced into another river system, the Atchafalaya.

This process helps keep the Mississippi from flooding. It also keeps the river from building new land, however.

Canals and other water control structures tame the river but cause long-term damage to delta wetlands

THE OLD DELTAS

The Mississippi has built seven deltas in the past 7,000 years. The river changes its final approach to the Gulf of Mexico roughly every thousand years. When the river fills its main channel with sediments, it finds a new course.

Over the years, the Mississippi delta changes size and shape. If the river does not flood and add new sediments, the delta shrinks. Ocean waves nibble away at the old delta land.

Riverboat traffic travels the Mississippi River's main channel from the Gulf of Mexico to New Orleans and points north

LIFE OF THE DELTA

The delta's wetlands are homes for hundreds of **species** (SPEE sheez), or kinds, of water-loving plants and animals.

Huge flocks of long-legged white **ibis** (I biss) and egrets live in the wetlands. Alligators float through the dark bayous to prey upon fish and turtles. A few black bears live in the swamps with muskrats, raccoons, minks, and otters.

One of the most important creatures of the wetlands is a miniature lobster, the crawfish.

White ibis high step into a blackwater delta swamp

CAJUN COUNTRY

The crawfish is a popular **Cajun** (KAY jun) food. The Cajuns in southern Louisiana are people whose ancestors were French Canadians. The Cajuns have kept many of their French customs.

Many delta people make their living from the land and water. Some are trappers or fishermen. Others harvest crawfish or raise alligators for their hides.

Delta farmers raise fruits, vegetables, sugar, and trees. Deep wells produce oil and natural gas.

A Cajun fisherman inspects a net he has made

THE DELTA TOMORROW

The delta country has changed in recent years. Much of the change has been the loss of wetlands and their resources.

Because of water control structures, the great river is no longer building the delta as it once did. The ocean has swallowed up thousands of acres of land and marshes. Now, many people in Louisiana are looking for ways to rebuild healthy marshes.

Louisiana's delta wetlands are important for wildlife and for the people whose jobs and way of life depend upon them.

Glossary

bayous (BUY youz) — slow-moving creeks or channels of water, especially in Louisiana, that connect with another body of water

Cajun (KAY jun) — in southern Louisiana, a person with some French Canadian ancestors

delta (DEL tuh) — the land—often in the shape of a rough triangle, like the Greek letter delta—deposited near a river's mouth by the river itself

ibis (I biss) — a slender, long-legged water bird with a long, down-curved bill

Mardi Gras (MAR de GRAH) — a festival of dances, parades, and parties that ends on the Tuesday (Mardi Gras Day) before the start of Lent; a festival brought to America by French settlers in the early 1700's

sediment (SEHD uh mint) — solid materials, such as clay and gravel, that may be carried by water currents

species (SPEE sheez) — a certain kind of animal within a closely related group; for example, a *brown* pelican

INDEX